Meal Prep for Weight Loss

Quick and easy low carb, vegan, vegetarian, vegetables recipes.
Recipes for weight loss with meal plan.
Instant pressure dishes.

The information in the following pages is broadly considered a truthful and accurate account of facts and as such, any inattention, use, or misuse of the information in question by the reader will render any resulting actions solely under their purview. There are no scenarios in which the publisher or the original author of this work can be in any fashion deemed liable for any hardship or damages that may befall them after undertaking information described herein.

Additionally, the information in the following pages is intended only for informational purposes and should thus be thought of as universal. As befitting its nature, it is presented without assurance regarding its prolonged validity or interim quality. Trademarks that are mentioned are done without written consent and can in no way be considered an endorsement from the trademark holder.

CONTENTS

STEP BY STEP INSTRUCTIONS TO BEAT A WEIGHT-LOSS PLATEAU—REALLY

Attempt these methodologies when your weight-loss endeavors feel like they're slowing down.

From the start, getting in shape felt practically simple. You assaulted your eating routine with conviction—reducing included sugar and increasing your vegetables. Working out was fun and individuals at the exercise center may have even begun to remember you. Dear companions give a shout out to you as those initial hardly any pounds appeared to slide directly off.

In any case, presently, months after the fact, not really. Truly, you're still dependably turning up at the exercise center and turning down treats. However, regardless of what you do, the scale is trapped. So what was the deal?

You've hit a weight-loss level, and it's not your issue. "Everybody is different, and a great deal relies upon how a lot of weight you need to lose, what plan you're on and different components—yet by and large, levels will in general strike after around a half year," says weight-loss master and certified fitness coach Melissa Majumdar, M.S., R.D., a representative for the Academy of Nutrition and Dietetics. Here's the means by which to push past the level and refocus to meet your weight-loss objectives.

Check Your Diet

Exercise assumes a fundamental job, as well—yet investigate demonstrates the way to enduring weight loss is the thing that you eat. These tips can assist you with busting through your level.

1. Track your nourishment.

Is it conceivable—quite possibly—that you're not adhering as near your eating routine as you might suspect? Chomps of one or the other can include and be difficult to pinpoint. The best way to know without a doubt is to record it, Majumdar says. She prescribes utilizing an application to effortlessly follow your admission. Or on the other hand you can generally write it down as our forefathers would have done it with pen and paper. However you pick, the outcomes may shock you and assist you with pulling together your endeavors.

2. Parity supplements.

You need protein for muscle development and fix, and healthy carbs for vitality. Check your nourishment log and see where you may be coming up short. Stick with lean wellsprings of protein like eggs, fish, chicken, Greek yogurt, beans, lentils and tofu. For carbs, go with entire grains like oats, dark colored rice, quinoa and farro, and starchier vegetables like sweet potatoes and butternut or spaghetti squash. Organic products are fine, as well—however watching your segments can be particularly useful as you're getting through this weight-loss level.

3. Plan meals.

Know early what, when and the amount you'll eat, Majumdar proposes. "Something else, the day escapes from you, and you wind up eating anything." Buy prechopped veggies to spare time in the kitchen, and check out one of EatingWell's Meal Plans, similar to our 7-Day, 1,200-Calorie Meal Plan.

4. Take a stab at something new.

Breaking out of a nourishment trench may assist you with breaking out of that level. "A large portion of us wear out on our go-to nourishments," Majumdar says. If you're tired of chicken bosom, have the thigh or drumstick rather or attempt another fish or tofu. Challenge yourself to attempt in any event one new formula every week.

5. Eat what you like.

"If you cut out the entirety of your preferred nourishments, the progressions won't last," Majumdar says. The stunt is making those old faves fit with your better approach for eating. If it's burgers you pine for, avoid the bun. Can't leave behind fries? Request them every so often, yet pair them with a serving of mixed greens. If you're a chocoholic, discover little approaches to fulfill your sweet tooth, as with one of these low-calorie chocolate pastries.

6. Remain savvy.

Edgy occasions—and your level may appear one—may in some cases appear to call for frantic measures, yet stick to healthy propensities. Try not to go underneath 1,200 calories every day without a specialist's supervision. "You need your craving and vitality levels to be supportable, and it's difficult to meet your day by day needs on such a restricted eating routine" Majumdar says.

7. Switch things up.

Your body becomes acclimated to a similar exercise, so after some time you won't see similar outcomes. Challenge yourself in different manners: if you've been doing for the most part cardio, include more quality preparing. "Weight lifting will be useful," says Majumdar. If you're found you may mass, unwind—specialists have put that fantasy to rest.

8. Increment power.

"This is the place I think many individuals have ridiculous desires," says Majumdar. "They'll include a walk, yet they don't get more fit, and they're disappointed." Try aerobics or different exercises that get your pulse up. "Practicing at greater force over brief timeframes can get you into weight-loss mode once more," she says.

9. Check your objectives.

Those early pounds you shed were in all probability water weight. From that point forward, weight loss normally eases back. Before you hurl out your restroom scale, ensure your objectives are reasonable. Ordinary weight loss is about a half-pound to two pounds per week, says Majumdar. If you're in that range, you may not be in such a droop all things considered.

10. Tally different triumphs.

We know it's hard, yet make an effort not to fixate on the numbers on the scale. Different changes tally, as well: Maybe you've lost an inch around your midsection, dropped a dress size or kicked your wellness level up a score. Get your blood checked and check whether your cholesterol has improved. Or on the other hand perhaps you've essentially seen you have more vitality nowadays. They're all motivations to celebrate!

11. Try not to whip yourself.

You and the posse went out to The Cheesecake Factory—and your eating routine vacated the premises. Skirt the blame. "Each plate is a fresh start," Majumdar says. "Settling on one terrible decision won't break your entire eating routine." Treat every meal as a crisp opportunity to settle on a healthy decision, and nix the negative self-talk.

12. Try not to surrender.

"Presumably the greatest slip-up calorie counters make is to stopped," says Majumdar. Rather, realize that you'll have to make alterations en route. "Your body changes, your life transforms," she includes. "So the first plan may not work. If you're not receptive, it will be all the more testing."

Weight-loss levels are a disappointing piece of the adventure, yet you can traverse. Discovering support from an exercise pal or online gathering—or from an expert—can help keep you responsible to get you over the end goal.

COULD LOSING WEIGHT SLOW YOUR METABOLISM?

Your body's digestion is often touted as the shrouded mystery of weight-loss achievement—a quick one encourages you get in shape, and a more slow one can neutralize you. In any case, can shedding pounds really make your digestion delayed down and turn drowsy?

If you've hit a weight-loss level you might be pondering, what gives? There's a lot of reasons weight loss may slow down out, however is your digestion hindering one of them?

Digestion gets a great deal of consideration around weight loss. It likewise gets a ton of pointless credit and fault. Your digestion is significant when it comes to weight, however it's not by any means the only factor at play. Here, we clarify the natural changes that happen to your digestion and your body during weight loss and what you can do about them.

What Is Metabolism?

Digestion alludes to the important substance forms that occur in your body so as to look after life.

Consider your body a vehicle. If you put gas in a vehicle, it utilizes that fuel so as to move. Similarly, your body utilizes calories from nourishment, or vitality, with the goal for it to move, inhale and work. Digestion is the procedure of your body using the vitality you put into it, or all the more just, consuming calories. You can likewise consume additional calories by including action, for example, strolling, moving or working out.

Your digestion incorporates these capacities that consume calories:

Basal or Resting Metabolic Rate (BMR or RMR): BMR alludes to how a lot of vitality (or what number of calories) your body consumes just to keep you alive. In any event, when you're sleeping, your body still uses vitality to siphon blood and keep your heart thumping.

Thermic Effect of Food (TEF): Your body needs vitality to process the nourishment you eat. The thermic impact of nourishment (TEF) incorporates the calories you consume processing nourishment. Along these lines, truly, eating consumes calories-in spite of the fact that the TEF is typically little and insufficient to exceed the calories you take in.

Non-Exercise Activity Thermogenesis (NEAT): NEAT alludes to the calories your body consumes every day exercises, for example, squirming, strolling to work, or going up the stairs.

What's the Difference between a Fast Metabolism and a Slow Metabolism?

A quick digestion is one that consumes a ton of calories to help its metabolic capacities. Your companions who can eat anything they desire without putting on weight likely have quick digestion systems. Interestingly, a moderate digestion doesn't consume the same number of calories to help the equivalent metabolic capacities.

You can reprimand hereditary qualities for this. "Numerous variables affect digestion including age, sex, hereditary qualities, body organization and weight," says Allison Knott, M.S., R.D.N., an enlisted dietitian situated in Brooklyn, New York. While hereditary qualities to a great extent decide what number of calories you consume doing different exercises, you do have some command over your metabolic rate.

Could Losing Weight Slow Your Metabolism?

Indeed, it can. If you eat less calories than you consume day by day exercises and exercise, you will get thinner. The crucial step is keeping up that weight loss. As a rule, somebody sheds pounds, keeps it off for some time and afterward recovers it. There are a few elements having an effect on everything during this procedure, and digestion is only one of them.

"When all is said in done, getting in shape prompts a lower resting metabolic rate and less calories consumed, including during movement," says Sarah Gold Anzlovar, M.S., R.D.N., L.D.N., organizer of Sarah Gold Nutrition. "Littler bodies require less vitality to work than a bigger body-simply like a little loft requires less vitality to warm than a bigger house."

You don't require the same number of calories to work at 150 pounds as you did at 200 pounds. Your BMR falls, or eases back, with weight loss.

To add to the disappointment, your mind additionally sends sign to your body that expansion hunger and decrease the quantity of calories you consume. Developmentally, this was a defensive system to prevent you from starving. Today it is a significant reason for weight recover.

This may appear to be discouraging, however you do have some command over the rate at which your digestion falls. You can prevent your digestion from easing back a lot by getting more fit gradually versus through an accident diet.

"If you go at abstaining from excessive food intake energetically your digestion falls, so it implies you lose less weight than the calories you cut," says Susan B. Roberts, Ph.D., senior researcher at the USDA Human Nutrition Research Center at Tufts and author of the online iDiet weight-loss program. "More slow eating less junk food has a littler impact. When you have shed pounds and balanced out, if you have been going at a moderate pace of one to two pounds for each week, there doesn't appear to be a long haul sway. Your digestion is lower because you are presently a littler individual, however not lopsidedly low."

Different Reasons Your Metabolism Can Slow Down

Weight loss isn't the main guilty party for a more slow digestion. If you eat too hardly any calories or go excessively long between meals (more than three or four hours), your digestion will back off. This is known as "starvation mode" and is because of the equivalent defensive instrument that happens when you get in shape. Your body hinders the rate at which it's consuming calories so as to preserve vitality, because it doesn't have the foggiest idea when you are going to bolster it once more. This is a one-two punch if you are seriously limiting calories to get thinner.

The proportion of fat to muscle in the body likewise influences metabolic rate. Weight, or body sythesis, is comprised of fat, muscle, bone and water. Muscle is more metabolically dynamic than fat. As it were, it consumes more calories. When you get more fit, you lose both fat and muscle, except if you are planning something for protect the bulk. Losing calorie-consuming slender bulk eases back your digestion.

"This is one motivation behind why you see an adjustment in digestion over the lifespan," Knott says. "As you age, you normally lose bulk, which brings about a diminished digestion. This can be affected by keeping up bulk all through the lifetime with weight-bearing physical action."

Could Your Metabolism Fall Below an "Ordinary" Level Because of Weight Loss?

There is no "ordinary" digestion. What is typical for you depends on your hereditary qualities, age, sex, weight and action level. In any case, what you consider typical for yourself can change after some time because of age, weight loss or muscle loss.

"Some more current research proposes that significant weight loss can prompt a lower metabolic rate than 'typical' for that weight and one that is reliably lower much after the weight is recaptured," Anzlovar says. "This implies if you began at 200 pounds and now weigh 150 pounds, you will consume less calories very still and during exercise than somebody who consistently weighed 150 pounds. What's considerably all the more disappointing for those that need to get thinner is that exploration has likewise demonstrated that if the individual who shed the 50 pounds recovers that weight, their digestion will be lower at 200 pounds than it was before the person lost the weight." It is indistinct if this consistently occurs or why it occurs, she included Would you be able to Boost Your Metabolism?

You may feel bound to the digestion you have, yet you can do a few things to keep your digestion fired up and keep it from backing off.

Eat all the more top notch nourishments. Adhere to an eating regimen with entire, natural nourishments, and eat them often. "Eating an extremely low-calorie diet or unnecessarily practicing and not eating enough often prompts a more slow digestion," Anzlovar says. Her customers are often shocked when she discloses to them they have to eat more. Eat each three to four hours to anticipate the starvation mode that advises your body to save vitality as opposed to consuming it.

Concentrate on protein and fiber. As indicated by Roberts, examine is progressing on the theme of digestion falling underneath a typical level. "Maybe higher-protein consumes less calories help avert the fall," she says. "Likewise, unquestionably higher-fiber diets will have a defensive impact." She and her associates found that when individuals with stable weights supplanted refined grains with entire grains, they had the option to humbly build their BMR (or RMR). That is the reason a high-fiber diet is the foundation of her weight-loss program. Different examinations affirm that eating nourishments high in protein and fiber and lower on the glycemic file lead to less yearning and more noteworthy degrees of completion, which help battle the expanded craving caused after weight loss. Expect to eat at any rate 25 to 35 grams of fiber for every day.

Get the weights. "Physical movement is one of only a handful not many ways that digestion can be significantly affected, both because being dynamic requires extra vitality and because of the shift in body piece," Knott says. Rather than concentrating just on cardio work out, include weight-bearing exercises as well. Cardio may give you a higher all out calorie consume, yet that implies you lose fat and muscle. Add a few days of solidarity preparing every week to help lose fat however protect muscle. "More bulk implies a better capacity to burn calories, so don't fear weight preparing," Anzlovar says.

Get going. Research shows that individuals who can keep weight off long haul practice near an hour consistently. The National Weight Control Registry, a database that pursues individuals who effectively shed pounds and keep it off, reports that 90 percent of their individuals practice for a normal of one hour of the day. Concentrates likewise show that individuals who consume every day practice however eat enough to keep up their weight can raise their metabolic rate. Roberts includes, "Exercise has a transient impact. For some time after you work out, your digestion is expanded. And afterward, long haul, the expansion in bulk you get from weights has a little impact."

Lamentably, getting in shape eases back your digestion, however you do have some control. Nix the accident diets, and work on changing propensities after some time. You will consume less calories as you get in shape and will probably be hungrier, yet you can counterbalance.

WEIGHT-LOSS TIPS THAT ACTUALLY WORK (ACCORDING TO SCIENCE)

The vast majority who attempt to get in shape mean well. They start solid, yet wind up losing steam and any weight they may have lost returns crawling. We investigated the most recent science to discover how individuals can really shed pounds the correct way and keep it off. Rather than crash abstaining from excessive food intake and consuming, here are 10 weight-loss tips that truly work.

1. Find a way to Lose Weight

You may have persuaded yourself that you can update your eating routine and start practicing each and every day, except that is somewhat similar to bouncing on a plane to Antarctica with no agenda. "You need a plan," says John Norcross, Ph.D., a therapist at the University of Scranton, who has examined New Year's goals. "What, specifically, are you going to do any other way?" Experts prescribe doing a cerebrum dump of the considerable number of changes you need to make, then beginning with one modest, feasible change pressing a healthy lunch or strolling 20 minutes every day. When that is an agreeable piece of your daily schedule, put an intense checkmark on your rundown, then include another little change. Without a doubt, gradual steps take longer, however they work: an ongoing report in the American Journal of Preventive Medicine found that individuals who rolled out one little improvement seven days lost almost twice as much weight as the individuals who pursued more extensive "eat less, move more" rules. Furthermore, envision how gratifying it will feel to see those checkmarks include as the pounds tumble off.

2. Keep Your Meals Simple

The less muddled confinements you have around your eating and working out, the better. You have to discover a plan or style of eating that works for you.

When specialists thought about ladies on two different eating regimen plans-one that gave weight watchers a rundown of nourishments they could eat and a couple of simple to-keep rules, and another increasingly entangled eating routine that permitted calorie counters more nourishment decisions, yet expected them to deliberately follow the entirety of their eating and exercise-they found that the individuals who found the last plan difficult were the well on the way to surrender. "Complex weight control plans can be difficult, so settle on one that appears to be reasonable," says study coauthor Peter Todd, Ph.D., an educator of psychological science and brain science at Indiana University in Bloomington and executive of the IU Food Institute. "Everybody has a different resilience, so the eating regimen that works for your closest companion may feel testing to you. Also, if you're feeling overpowered by an eating regimen, change to a more straightforward methodology. That is obviously better than stopping inside and out."

3. Set Two Goal Weights

If you have a major long haul objective to lose at least 20 pounds, it very well may be useful to celerbate the littler strides en route.

Let's be honest: the possibility of shedding 20 pounds-or more-is overwhelming. That is the reason Rachel Beller, M.S., R.D.N., creator of Eat to Lose, Eat to Win, suggests defining a closer term objective weight that is around half of the aggregate sum you need to lose-and concentrating on that. "Having a simpler to-arrive at objective can help keep you persuaded," she says. "What's more, when you hit that first achievement, it allows you to commend, rethink your technique and re-up your excitement for the following stage."

4. Eat Your Vegetables First

Analysts at the University of Minnesota did a progression of concentrates in which they had members eat vegetables before they put some other nourishment on their plates-and even the specialists were shocked by what they found. "Individuals expended up to multiple times more veggies than expected," says Traci Mann, Ph.D., who drove the examination. What's more, members who chomped carrots before being offered M&Ms in this way ate 33% less treat than the individuals who were simply given the sweet first. For what reason does this stunt work? Because when any nourishment is placed before us, we for the most part let it all out and the veggies aren't rivaling different food sources on our plate (which we will in general go for first, if given the choice). So start with a plate of mixed greens or crudités.

Also, spare the bread for the finish of the meal. Eating basic carbs first drastically builds glucose, which makes your body siphon out insulin and store the calories as fat something contrary to what you need if you're attempting to shed pounds, says heftiness master Louis Aronne, M.D., a teacher of metabolic research at Weill Cornell Medical College. "Having a few vegetables and protein before straightforward carbs blunts that unhealthy glucose reaction," he includes.

5. Solace Food Won't Actually Comfort You

In the relatively recent past, Traci Mann and her partners demonstrated examination subjects a pitiful motion picture, then enabled some of them to eat their preferred feel-better nourishment, for example, brownies, treats and dessert. Others were given a granola bar, while a third gathering ate nothing by any stretch of the imagination. When the analysts evaluated their subjects' states of mind a short time later, there was no difference among the three gatherings. At the end of the day, brownies aren't the surefire shot in the arm we think they are. Mann's takeaway: "When you feel terrible, you're far superior off calling a companion or taking a walk-the two of which are demonstrated to lift temperament." These alternatives additionally have zero calories.

6. Make Peace with the Scale

If the restroom scale is an instrument of torment to you, it's an ideal opportunity to make harmony! Studies show that individuals who effectively get thinner and keep it off long haul gauge themselves routinely. Else you're in danger of thoughtlessly recapturing. In one examination, 33% of ladies didn't understand they'd put on five pounds through the span of a half year and a quarter did not understand they'd increased nine. To get over your scale fear, advise yourself that the number isn't a prosecution of you as an individual, says Dawn Jackson Blatner, R.D.N. "Consider it target information like the temperature on an open air thermometer-that can give you supportive data about whether you're on track with your eating regimen," she says. Furthermore, every day weighing may be ideal. "It demystifies the scale and removes a portion of its capacity," clarifies Carly Pacanowski, Ph.D., R.D., who has directed weighing-recurrence learns at Cornell University.

7. Abbreviate Your Eating Window

A progression of new investigations recommends that when you eat might be as significant as what you eat. In one, members who ordinarily ate inside a 15-hour window were advised to limit it to 10 or 11 hours-and they dropped a normal of seven pounds over the 16-week study, without transforming whatever else about their eating. "The planning of nourishment consumption influences the body's inward clock, which thusly influences qualities that assume a job in digestion," says study creator Satchidananda Panda, Ph.D., a partner teacher at the Salk Institute for Biological Studies in San Diego. As such, our bodies may consume calories all the more productively when we eat during a shorter window of the day. So consider having your morning meal somewhat later and your supper somewhat prior.

8. Watch Which Foods You Put in Your Grocery Cart

Your buys may not be as prudent as you might suspect. Analysts from the University of North Carolina at Chapel Hill as of late broke down Americans' shopping propensities and found that 61 percentof the calories in the nourishment we purchase are from profoundly prepared things like refined breads, treats, wafers, pop and chips. These nourishments likewise give higher-than-ideal degrees of soaked fat, sugar and sodium. To healthy-up your truck and help with weight loss, the investigation creators recommend purchasing for the most part single-fixing nourishments and shopping the border of the store, where the fresher, healthier stuff like produce and fish will in general live. Bite some gum while you're grinding away as well. Research shows it could assist you with purchasing 7 percent less low quality nourishment when you shop (minty gum works best).

9. Stop the Negative Self-Talk

Ugh, I'm so fat! For a considerable lot of us, that is the thing that goes for a weight-loss motivational speech. "There's this basic misguided judgment that being no picnic for yourself is the best way to accomplish your objectives," says Kristin Neff, Ph.D., partner teacher of human improvement at the University of Texas at Austin and creator of Self-Compassion. But treating yourself with thoughtfulness, inquire about shows, is a superior method to support your duty to healthy practices. "Mentor yourself through your good and bad times the manner in which you'd mentor a companion with uplifting statements and backing," says Neff. "For example, if you indulge or increase a couple of pounds, let yourself know, 'Getting thinner is hard for everybody I'm not by any means the only one battling. I'm going to take it gradually and keep at it.'" Think of consistently even every meal-as a chance to begin once again.

10. Try not to Expect Weight Loss to Be Easy

Investigations of effective calorie counters uncover a hard truth: "They remain genuinely severe about their eating always," says James O. Slope, Ph.D., fellow benefactor of the National Weight Control Registry, which keeps information on a great many individuals who have shed pounds and kept it off. Sound discouraging? Consider it along these lines, proposes Eat to Lose, Eat to Win creator Beller: "You simply need to locate a dietary methodology you can live with long haul like enabling yourself to have dessert or a mixed drink or two now and again. It resembles moving to another city. For the main year or so it's difficult, yet once you build up a standard you get settled. You may in any case miss things about your previous lifestyle, yet you're content with your new one as well."

VIRTUOSO TRICKS FOR FREEZING FOOD THAT'LL MAKE MEAL PREP A SNAP

Reality: such stands among you and interminable additional money, reduced nourishment squander, and quick access to pre-prepared suppers you don't need to cook is your cooler. Everybody claims one, yet almost certainly, you aren't utilizing yours the correct way—or to its maximum capacity. We counseled with Matt Davis and Sam McIntire, fellow benefactors of Mosaic, a game-changing present day solidified meal conveyance administration, to get their master intel on the best way to appropriately solidify crisp nourishments and remains.

Keep away from nourishments with fresh and crunchy surfaces.

The fresh breading on nourishment like seared chicken or chicken parm will in general corrupt when defrosted in the microwave. Soups, stews, and sauces, then again, keep up their flavor and consistency for an ideal defrost.

Stop nourishments quick.

The quicker veggies solidify, the greater they'll be when defrosted. Subsequent to cooking vegetables, give laying them a shot on a sheet skillet in your cooler as opposed to bunching them up in a heap (this is called 'IQFing,' or individual speedy solidifying). They'll solidify quicker and keep up their generous broiled surface when warmed.

Use sacks for soup.

If you make a huge bunch of custom made juices, solidify the remains in cooler packs to have close by for future soups or braising. They're shockingly sealed shut and won't hoard so a lot of room inside your cooler as plastic compartments do.

Avoid thick bits of protein.

They often defrost unevenly, and nobody prefers that out of the blue chilly first nibble.

Stop crisp produce at its pinnacle.

Keep your rancher's market finds new. Stocking up and solidify in-season things is an extraordinary method to approach products of the soil when they might be out of season and progressively costly to purchase new.

Leave room at the top.

When solidifying fluids (like juices, milk, or squeeze), try to leave room at the highest point of the compartment for the fluid to grow. If not, be set up for a cooler profound clean.

Continuously permit enough time for defrosting.

If you realize you need to make burgers for your Saturday BBQ, move the meat to the cooler two or three days ahead of time. Defrosting in a microwave can too effectively cook as opposed to defrost the meat, and forgetting about nourishment to defrost on the counter can make it risky to eat.

If appearance matters to you, whiten greens first.

Green sauces, similar to pesto, will darken normally as they're presented to the air in your cooler. They're still splendidly safe to eat, however have a go at whitening (heating up) your greens before making your sauce, which will slow the darkening procedure for a more brilliant, greener solidified sauce.

Try not to hurl extra herbs.

Rather, transform them into moment enhance 3D shapes. When a formula requires a limited quantity of a herb yet you have a whole pack left, cut up the rest, add them to an ice plate and spread with oil and stop. Whenever you're sautéing or broiling a dish, toss in a couple of these 3D shapes for included flavor.

Propelled Meal Prep Tips and Tricks

Plan Your Meals

Preparing more meals at home is useful for your health and your wallet. With a bit of planning, you can fit it into even the busiest week. The objective is to capitalize on the time you spend in the kitchen. Start by posting your meals for the week ahead, and be specific. You could even make a fundamental blueprint for every week: stew on Monday, pasta on Thursday, and tacos on Friday. It can make planning simpler, and a few people, particularly kids, such as comprehending what's in store.

Start straightforward. Turkey bean stew and cooked vegetables are a snap to make and warm effectively. Lasagna or fish stew, then again, take more work and may not remain as new. When you discover a formula that looks great, spare it in a document or spreadsheet. When you make your picks, make a rundown of every fixing to purchase, including the amount you need. Applications and other online devices can assist you with making sense of careful sums.

Pick Versatile Ingredients

Search for nourishments that work in a couple of different dishes. For instance, you may utilize quinoa to make a side dish, add to a serving of mixed greens, or as a major aspect of a grain bowl for lunch. A dish chicken can be an entrée, added to a soup, or served in tacos consistently. What's more, if there's any left finished, you can solidify it.

Shop Once

When you have your rundown, pick a shopping day that accommodates your timetable. Possibly you like heading off to the local ranchers advertise on Saturdays or hitting up the supermarket on a weeknight when it's not occupied. Make certain to purchase exactly what you need. What's more, don't give seeing seven days of staple goods a chance to overpower you when you return home. Keep in mind, you don't need to shop and cook around the same time.

Pick a Prep Day

Preparing more nourishment without a moment's delay makes it simpler to assemble healthy meals on chaotic days. Pick a day of every week to prepare the same number of your dishes as you can. Furthermore, make it fun! Put on some music. Welcome a companion over to share the work and the nourishment. Or on the other hand transform it into a family undertaking - everybody finds a new line of work that matches their age. If meals for an entire week appear to be excessive to take on, start with 2 or 3 days' worth and prep another dish later in the week.

Consider Cooking Time

On prep day, start with nourishments that need the most time on the stove or in the broiler: cooking meat, simmering vegetables, dousing or stewing beans, making quinoa. When you have those pots and dish going, you can do snappier errands like washing lettuce or cleaving carrots and celery into helpful bite sizes. If you don't prefer to pre-cook your meat, put it in a marinade so it's prepared to hurl into the skillet or stove when you need it.

Keep the Basics on Hand

A couple "go-to" nourishments are in every case great to have in the house for a tidbit or to add to a meal: Nuts and seeds, washed greens, hard-bubbled eggs, slashed natural product. Convenient solution nourishments that keep for quite a while are likewise great, similar to rice, dried pasta, canned fish, and solidified veggies. They make it simple to toss something together, in any event, when you haven't been to the store in some time.

Make Extra

If you realize you utilize a great deal of certain fixings or plans, twofold or triple the sum you cook on the double. You can spare yourself the problem of cooking beans, bubbling eggs, or steaming veggies a few evenings for each week.

Segment It Out

Gap huge plans into all set single servings, and you may spare yourself some time during the week. It can likewise prevent you from eating excessively. Put each serving in a re-sealable plastic sack or glass holder. You can likewise pour soups, stews, and stocks into silicone biscuit tins, solidify them, and pop the pieces into a plastic pack after they solidify.

A Trick for Veggies

You can "whiten" your vegetables - dunk them in bubbling water and rapidly cool them - to make them last longer in the cooler. Reward: it likewise lights up their shading, seals in taste and nutrients, and disposes of germs. Wash them off and slice them to the correct size before you start this procedure.

Lunch in a Jar

You can pre-make five without a moment's delay and eat all week. Put nuts, grains, protein, and dressing at the base of a 8-ounce container, with veggies and greens on top. Or on the other hand make a "wrap-less" burrito with beans, rice, and veggies. Another thought: partition out single-serve smoothie fixings that are prepared to toss in the blender.

Remain Organized

When you have things prepared and pressed, don't lose it all in the rear of your ice chest or cooler. Mark every holder with the substance and the date. Keep the stuff that has been there longer close to the front so you use it first. Put nourishment that turns sour quickest, similar to herbs and slashed organic product, at eye level so you remember about them.

Useful for How Long?

Try not to give your difficult work a chance to ruin in the ice chest! Remember to what extent a few nourishments will remain great refrigerated:

Ground meat or chicken (cooked): 1-2 days

Entire meats, poultry, fish, soups, and stews (cooked): 3-4 days

Beans, chickpeas (cooked): 5 days

Hard bubbled eggs, hacked vegetables: multi week

Delicate cheddar (opened): 2 weeks

Hard cheddar (opened): 5 a month and a half

Stop!

Sealed shut compartments are best for solidifying nourishment. You can spare space if you utilize enormous re-sealable plastic packs and crush out any additional air. Anything will solidify, yet nourishments with heaps of water, similar to serving of mixed greens or tomatoes, don't generally function admirably. When you store them, remember to what extent they'll remain great:

Soups, stews, beans (cooked): 2-3 months

Ground meat, poultry (cooked): 3-6 months

Apples, bananas, pears, plums, mangoes, berries: 6-8 months

Vegetables: 8 a year

THE BEST MEAL PREP AND DIET PLAN FOR WEIGHT LOSS

The Best Meal Prep and Diet Plan for Weight Loss won't limit you from getting a charge out of life – actually, it's tied in with being adaptable and appreciating healthy eating as a lifestyle! I'll tell you the best way to meal prep for weight loss without being on a severe eating routine.

Meal Prep for Weight Loss

When you're meal preparing just because, you may see that you wind up getting in shape because you're eating healthier and are progressively arranged for meal time. I've been meal preparing on and off for as far back as 5 years and it's been a key segment of self-consideration that has had some entirely astonishing advantages.

I've set aside quite a lot of money throughout the years by having healthy snacks arranged for the work week (read progressively about how to eat healthy on a financial limit), and because of being increasingly sorted out with my meals, I've improved my general health and have additionally lost some weight while doing it!

Is Meal Prepping Good for Weight Loss?

You can meal prep and experience weight loss.

Whenever you remain sorted out and control your bits of nourishment, you are grabbing eat healthier, and this may bring about weight loss.

You are likewise more effectively ready to figure the carbohydrate content because you have prepared the nourishment yourself and skill numerous parts are in a formula and how to separate that formula into the proper segment size. I have healthful data on the entirety of my plans and most other nourishment sites offer something very similar.

If you know precisely what you're eating and when, it will help with any kind of weight loss plan. Additionally, if you have nourishment available that you have arranged for the week you are less inclined to have out at lunch or request takeout after work, and you are likewise less inclined to nibble because when you're ravenous, the nourishment is in that spot hanging tight for you.

Do You Have to Meal Prep to Lose Weight?

Presently, I realize I may have persuaded you that meal preparing is THE best approach to shed pounds, yet you unquestionably don't need to meal prep to encounter weight loss.

For whatever length of time that you are encountering a type of calorie shortage, you will get thinner. Meal prep can enable you to control what you're eating and furthermore prevent you from being enticed to "cheat", however as long as you are preparing healthy nourishment and are following what you're eating, you will get more fit.

I will say that you do need to have a type of objective as a primary concern and an essential comprehension of what calorie admission will be fitting to accomplish those objectives.

What number of Calories Should You Eat?

Things being what they are, we gone to the deep rooted inquiry then: what number of calories would it be advisable for you to eat?

Indeed, the appropriate response is that it truly depends. It's for the most part dependent on your sex, tallness, weight, age and action level – read progressively about calorie tallying and weight loss here.

As an essential principle, you ought to eat between 1200-1700 calories per day so as to get thinner relying upon the variables I recorded previously. If you are dynamic, then you ought to presumably even be eating somewhat more. You can compute the measure of calories you ought to eat every day to keep up your weight and you can likewise ascertain the calories for weight loss so you have a thought of how your body is working.

One of the most widely recognized misinterpretations about weight loss is that you need to starve yourself or limit what you're eating yet now and again this can disturb your digestion and cause your body to go into starvation mode and clutch all the fat you're putting away. You'll likewise likely be really hopeless.

It's significant that you feed yourself enough to be solid and have a lot of vitality for the duration of the day. You'll additionally need to eat entire nourishments that you discover flavorful so as to encounter weight loss in a healthy and pleasurable way. If you take a reasonable, manageable methodology then it's absolutely conceivable!

The entirety of this stated, I genuinely don't put an excess of accentuation on calorie tallying because it very well may be difficult to do – it's normally unsustainable over the long haul and keeping in mind that it was something I accomplished for a piece while I had a weight loss objective, I just truly adhered to it for four months and after that I had a decent gauge of the measure of calories I was eating every day. You will inevitably have the option to eyeball how a lot of chicken you are eating, for example, and what number of calories each serving of nourishment is.

When I made sense of this all, my accentuation turned out to be less on getting in shape and tallying calories and more on encouraging myself healthy nourishments, eating carefully and supporting my body with the goal that I can be solid, healthy and cheerful.

You additionally need to be cautious with calorie checking and perceive if it isn't useful for you because it can in some cases cause you to shape an awful association with nourishment.

The amount Weight Will You Lose?

Once more, this is difficult to state yet it relies upon your objectives!

For me actually, I just never feel as if it's a smart thought going into meal prep with the possibility that you will lose a TON of weight. I went from 140lbs to 115lbs, yet I'm 5'2" and genuinely dainty. I am as of now 122-125lbs relying upon the day – this is by all accounts the typical range that my body likes to remain at and I have acknowledged this just like something to be thankful for.

Weight loss can be the same amount of mental as it is physical so you need to set yourself up for the way that you are as yet going to probably sit inside a specific scope of weight and that is alright! Magnificence comes in all shapes and sizes so it's imperative to perceive that as you are defining your objectives.

I feel that whenever you set a weight loss objective, you should be practical about how much weight you want to lose and what amount is vital. Toward the day's end, weight loss ought to be more for health reasons than vanity purposes and you ought to consistently attempt to concentrate on eating carefully and tuning in to your body. That is the place you will have the most achievement.

The more extended that you stay with a standard that empowers to you cook more at home and make progressively healthy meals that attention on entire nourishment fixings, the more weight you will have the option to lose – and once more, this truly relies upon how a lot of weight you believe you need to lose in any case.

In my very own case, I didn't feel as if I needed to lose a lot of weight. I wasn't even overweight. I was slightly heavier than I regularly am and my emphasis on a healthy eating regimen and wellness had melted away while I was in school. I needed to return to a healthier lifestyle and at first set a weight loss objective of 20lbs. I feel as if I had the option to lose that weight in an overly healthy manner and once I accomplished that objective I was glad to simply keep up my weight without concentrating on eating a lower calorie diet yet eating healthy nourishments.

To what extent Does Food Stay Good When You Meal Prep?

The greater part of the meal prep plans you'll discover recorded beneath will toward the end in the cooler for 4-6 days.

That is the ideal measure of time for you to take every one of your snacks to work every day of the work week just as appreciate a few scraps on days when you're too occupied to even think about cooking!

You can likewise in some cases broaden the timeframe of realistic usability of your nourishment by meal preparing separate fixings or slashing veggies and meat independently then cooking new. You will discover what works for you after some time as you keep on meal prep and see what you have to make ahead versus what you would prefer to appreciate new.

Shouldn't something be said about Freezer Meals?

Cooler meal prep plans will last significantly more – as long as 3 months or more! The key with cooler meal prep is discovering plans that will stop and afterward warm well. It's increasingly difficult to solidify cooked veggies and chicken and still get a similar taste and quality as when it's a crisp meal.

Things like pastas, soups, stews, smaller than usual pizzas and dishes solidify truly well however, just as some morning meal things like oatmeal cups and egg nibbles.

Once more, as referenced before with preparing separate fixings, you can likewise solidify natural products (or make smoothie packs!) and vegetables alongside things like cooked rice and pasta to make your life somewhat simpler when you do go to prepare new meals during the week.

How Do I Start a Meal Plan to Lose Weight?

Meal planning is in reality exceptionally easy to do once you begin, and it's the way to meal preparing in a sorted out manner. While you don't really should be on an eating regimen plan for weight loss, it helps to plan out what you will eat and when with the goal that you have the correct structure to remain on track. It will likewise truly rouse you to accomplish your objectives! I commonly advocate for plans to be in the middle of 300 to 500 calories when you are hoping to encounter weight loss because they are appropriate for a 1500-calorie daily diet. Once more, this is only an estimated benchmark that will apply to numerous individuals, myself notwithstanding, yet certainly not all. You can peruse more on why a 1500 calorie daily diet generally works for weight loss here. You ought to utilize the mini-computers referenced above to assist you with deciding how much weight you'd prefer to lose also. Setting is everything!

For instance, if we were following a 1500-calorie daily diet, then three meals per day at 400 calories each would approach 1200 calories, then you would have around 300 calories apportioned for snacks for the duration of the day also (suppose two snacks at 150 calories each). I would state you should in any case be eating around four or five times each day including your tidbits however once more, this specific eating routine plan is the thing that worked best for me.

Whenever you start a "diet", you should factor in what is reasonable for your present lifestyle. I truly support a general lifestyle change so as to accomplish dependable weight loss results – an accentuation on eating entire nourishments and healthy fixings. Dispose of the bundled nourishments and cook healthy meals at home. This is the place meal prep helps as a component of an eating regimen plan!

The entirety of the above considered, here is an extremely basic blueprint of what an eating routine plan may resemble for you in a day:

Meal 1: 300-400 calorie breakfast. I will ordinarily go with a cut of egg white frittata and a large portion of a bagel, or a hotdog egg Mcmuffin.

Meal 2: 100 calorie nibble, eaten toward the beginning of the day. Normally a banana, a large portion of an apple and 1 tbsp of nutty spread, a small Greek yogurt, or veggies and 2 tbsp hummus

Meal 3: 400 calorie lunch. I love meal prep bowls like this Greek chicken or this wild ox chicken wrap

Meal 4: 200 calorie nibble, eaten toward the evening. Possibly a protein bar (custom made like these protein chomps or locally acquired), s0me salted peanuts or almonds, cold cuts or turkey pepperettes, and more organic product and veggies

Meal 5: 400 calorie supper. I love this pesto chicken or these sheet container chicken fajitas – both are straightforward meals that meet up rapidly yet at the same time pack a huge amount of flavor!

If you need a little treat toward the day's end, shave a few calories off of your meals (possibly eat 350 calorie meals rather than 400 calories or make breakfast lower in calories alone). You can likewise eat lower calorie bites, or sub in dessert by the day's end for your morning nibble. You generally have some squirm room and adaptability even while following an eating routine plan.

The key is to not limit yourself or build up an unhealthy fixation on nourishment and checking calories. You should in any case have the option to eat the nourishments you like with some restraint and have some good times at parties! Continuously recall that destitute yourself won't help with weight loss so get out there and keep on making the most of your life. Weight loss requires some investment, consistency, and a healthy outlook.

If you'd like even more a well-spread out meal prep plan for weight loss, here is another wonderful 7-day meal prep plan to help with your objectives!

Meal Prep Recipes for Weight Loss

Here are a portion of my top meal prep plans – they are all between 300-500 calories so you can guarantee that they're healthy and will assist you with adhering to whatever weight loss objectives you have as a main priority.

I suggest beginning with a couple of the accompanying plans and adding them to your meal plan. When you're open to cooking more at home, you can generally make more plans and change up your eating regimen!

APPROACHES TO CURE AN UNHEALTHY RELATIONSHIP WITH FOOD

It is safe to say that you are terrified to have a treat because you may eat the entire box? Do you tally calories throughout the day, then gorge before bed? If you fixate on what you put in your mouth (and who doesn't?), here's the means by which to end the frenzy. I ought to have run over yonder and gulped down my treat with free satisfaction. Yet, I asked off. The idea of eating a sauce-shrouded heap of sugar and fat gave me a shock of blame and disgrace. I hadn't entered the store, and I was at that point loaded with lament.

It's terrible being in a useless association with nourishment. I would contrast it with lamentable hookups with failures from quite a while ago, yet those excursions didn't keep going extremely long. Nourishment and I have been separating and making up since youth.

The most exceedingly terrible part? Our issue is totally uneven. A cheeseburger doesn't realize I exist. My affections for a cheeseburger, in any case, are entangled. In any case, in spite of the fact that I'm a ceaseless weight watcher, my dietary patterns are viewed as typical. I don't have a clinical issue like bulimia or anorexia. I basically need to be slender and healthy.

Also, I'm not by any means the only one, in light of my companions, the smash hit records and the clique of Whole Foods. We live in a world in which we realize self-starvation is terrible, yet by one way or another think drinking just squeeze is great. "Our fixation on appearance, our obsession with diet and our nourishment and data copious culture have offered ascend to a scourge of unhealthy associations with nourishment," says Michelle May, MD, creator of Eat What You Love, Love What You Eat. "Nourishment has become our concentration as opposed to being the fuel for a full life."

To facilitate the choke hold your eating routine has over you, think about shouldn't something be said about it leaves you so frail. Look at the accompanying guilty parties. Odds are, you can identify with in any event one—if not all—of them.

Issue No. 1: You're managed by rules

A healthy sentimental association rotates around bargain. A few ladies, however, treat nourishment like they would an eccentric young doggie—something to be taught. Ann, a picture taker in New York City, keeps a rundown of nourishment manages on her ice chest. "Only a couple," she says. "No sugar, no white or seared nourishment, no dairy, no gluten and no carbonation. I do eat hamburger." A companion from Orlando gathers a different bag for her protein bars when she goes to ensure she won't be enticed by questionable lodging contributions. On an ongoing excursion, there was an issue about bringing nourishment into a nation. She went crazy at migration, fumed insanely and cried. The authorities were so stunned, they let her keep her bars.

This sort of inflexibility is about dread of losing control, says Susan Albers, PsyD, writer of 50 Ways to Soothe Yourself Without Food. "Our brains love to think in high contrast terms," Albers brings up. "Right versus wrong. Fat versus slim. Immaculate versus demolished." Or that is the manner by which it may appear when in the throes of a fixation. "A few people feel lost without structure," includes Mary Pritchard, PhD, educator in the branch of brain science at Boise State University. "Strolling into an eatery or opening an ice chest commences a calculation of tallying."

These musings aren't constrained to type As, however. They're on a psychological circle in a considerable lot of our heads, because of an over-burden of (often clashing) data about what we ought to and shouldn't eat. What's more, except if you hint into this craving for dietary flawlessness, you can do genuine harm to your confidence. "When you defy a norm, that can winding into 'I'm an awful individual,'" Albers notes. "Be that as it may, nourishment isn't positive or negative. There are 50 shades in the middle. Rule-based eating doesn't consider appetite and longings."

Also, that sets you up for a fall when your stomach begins protesting and you're compelled to go amiss from your well-laid eating plans. Rather than staying with a routine, attempt to be somewhat less severe. "I urge ladies to eat a wide assortment of nourishments," Albers says. "It's healthier from a nourishing and enthusiastic point of view." obviously, that is a lot more difficult than one might expect. A half-advance: Every day, disrupt your guidelines, a tad. "Start little," she asks. "A bit of bread. Pasta once every week. When you see that nothing awful occurs, adaptability won't be as scary. You may even appreciate it."

Issue No. 2: You don't confide in yourself

Another given in a healthy relationship is trust—trusting you and your accomplice will make the best choice when looked with allurement. In a broken "foodship"— as I like to call it—doubt can be uncontrolled. I realize I am frail around cake, for example. To prevent from eating excessively, I have drenched prepared products in water. A companion let me know, "I utilize hot sauce." Another: "Fluid cleanser."

My companion Rachel from New Jersey has a full best stuff. "I utilize a clock between chomps," she clarifies. "When I'm set, I solidify the scraps so I won't eat them. My sweetheart is accountable for doling out snacks under the guidance that he can't give me more than my apportioning, regardless of whether I ask."

It's not our shortcoming that it's so difficult to oppose chips and sweet. It's plain science: Eating starches (plentiful in pizza and cupcakes, however less in kale) supports our degrees of the vibe great hormone serotonin. Furthermore, we may have cheerful youth relationship with specific treats. No big surprise that a few of us hunger for comfort nourishment when we're vexed, exhausted, forlorn, etcetera. Stress triggers a jones for sugar; treats are promptly accessible. If you make an effort not to consider the treat, your mind just becomes focused. So when you at long last purchase the treats, you're too fixated to even think about stopping at only one (or three).

If we were progressively aware of craving prompts, however, we'd settle on better options. "Prior to eating, interruption to ask yourself, Does my body need fuel? For what reason am I thinking about nourishment if my body needn't bother with it?" Dr. May says. If you do need to eat, tune in to your yearnings: Indulging a little presently can prevent you from trying too hard later, Dr. May notes. Concerning the amount to eat, your body can help with that, as well. "The perfect sum is tied in with feeling better," Dr. May says, and not awkwardly stuffed a short time later.

Issue No. 3: You Beat Yourself Up

Envision having a beau who, after you committed a little error, called you a useless disappointment. You'd dump his butt. Be that as it may, a considerable lot of us do something very similar to ourselves if we set out to appreciate a bit of cake. "The nourishment as-foe voice disgraces you for overindulging," Albers says. "The nourishment as-companion voice is a team promoter. If you mess up, it urges you to refocus."

To quietness your internal bitch, steer dim nourishment musings to the light. When you're being exacting—I'm a disappointment. Everybody believes I'm fat—stop and tune in to what you're stating to yourself. Then supplant the destructive message with a benevolent one, similar to No one's ideal. My loved ones love me. After some time, this will get regular.

Discussing loved ones, do yours incorporate weight watchers who are considerably more basic than you are? They're not making a difference. Your optimal eating friends: "Individuals who eat gradually and enjoy their nourishment," Albers says.

Issue No. 4: You outrageously need to be thin

A healthy relationship is straightforward. An unhealthy one is loaded with trickiness. I realize I deceived myself during an ongoing juice quick. I said I was doing it for the cancer prevention agents. Bull! I needed to get thinner. "The main source of nourishment confinement is body disappointment," Pritchard says. "90% of ladies don't care for what they find in the mirror."

There's nothing amiss with needing to be thin. Be that as it may, denying yourself of critical supplements (or eating just a chosen few)— regardless of whether through purifies, fasts or removing nutrition types—and imagining it's in support of the benefit of your health is a perilous game. Unexpectedly, it can reverse discharge and set off the "starve, gorge, despise yourself" cycle that makes you put on weight.

And all that negative self-talk is no formula for weight loss, either. I realize that when I'm more pleasant to myself, I will in general eat better and keep up a weight that is healthier for my body—and my mental soundness. "In our way of life, so much is driven by shallow impression of what's beneficial," Dr. May says. "By fixating on weight loss, we're not accomplishing what we're prepared to do. It's swarming out stuff that is progressively significant"— like our joy and prosperity. I'll eat to that.

MEAL PREP RECIPES TO HELP YOU LOSE WEIGHT

Meal prep can assist you with getting more fit by setting you up for progress. When you have a healthy plan set up you're more averse to snatch take-out and prepared nourishments on the run. Here are EatingWell's best meal-prep plans for weight loss that are wealthy in veggies, organic products, entire grains, healthy protein and fat to assist you with arriving at your weight loss objectives in a healthy manner.

Green Veggie Bowl with Chicken and Lemon-Tahini Dressing

For this healthy 30-minute supper, treat your veggies like pasta and cook until still somewhat firm, or simply done. If you have some additional time, twofold or triple the lemon-tahini dressing and use it to rapidly dress a serving of mixed greens or as a sauce for steak or shrimp.

Fixings 4 servings

¼ cup tahini ¼ cup cold water in addition to 2 tablespoons, separated ¼ cup lemon juice ½ teaspoon minced garlic in addition to 2 cut garlic cloves, partitioned ¼ teaspoon ground cumin ½ teaspoon genuine salt, isolated 1 cup green beans 1 little broccoli crown (4 ounce) chicken cutlets, cut ¼ teaspoon ground pepper 2 tablespoons extra-virgin olive oil, isolated ½ enormous red onion, cut 4 cups meagerly cut kale 2 cups cooked dark colored rice ¼ cup slashed new cilantro

Planning

Whisk tahini and ¼ cup water in a little bowl until smooth. Include lemon juice, minced garlic, cumin and ¼ teaspoon salt and race to consolidate. Put in a safe spot. Trim green beans and cut down the middle. Break broccoli into florets. Measure 1 cup (hold the rest for another utilization). Season chicken with the remaining ¼ teaspoon salt and pepper. Warmth 1 tablespoon oil in an enormous cast-iron skillet over medium warmth. Include the chicken and cook until a moment read thermometer registers 160°F, 3 to 5 minutes for each side. Move to a perfect cutting board and tent with foil to keep warm. Crash the skillet and include the staying 1 tablespoon oil. Include onion and cook, mixing once in a while, for 2 minutes. Include cut garlic and cook for 30 seconds, then include the broccoli and green beans. Cook, mixing periodically, for 2 minutes. Mix in kale and include the staying 2 tablespoons water. Spread and steam until the vegetables are delicate fresh, 1 to 2 minutes. Cut the chicken. To serve, separate rice and the vegetables among 4 dishes and top with the chicken. Shower with the saved dressing and sprinkle with cilantro.

To make ahead: Refrigerate dressing (Step 1) for as long as 3 days.

Power Greens Salad with Baked Tofu and Honey-Mustard Vinaigrette

This plant-based fundamental dish serving of mixed greens sneaks up all of a sudden of greens, supplements and flavor. Include healthy protein with advantageous prepared tofu cuts, which have a firm surface that is appropriate to servings of mixed greens and sandwiches. Sprinkle on a little mash with fragmented almonds, and only a trace of tropical sweetness with unsweetened coconut. The vinaigrette balances the dish with tart sweet kick.

Fixings 1 serving

2 cups Power Greens Salad (see related formula) 4 ounces heated tofu, cut into ½-inch-thick cuts 2 tablespoons fragmented almonds, toasted 2 tablespoons unsweetened coconut 2 tablespoons Honey-Mustard Vinaigrette (see related formula).

Arrangement

Pack plate of mixed greens in a water/air proof stockpiling compartment or huge artisan container. Include tofu, almonds and coconut. Pack vinaigrette independently in a little container. Just before eating, add the vinaigrette to the serving of mixed greens and hurl to cover.

Chicken Burrito Bowls with Sweet Potato Rice

Tired of cauliflower "rice" yet searching for a low-carb swap for normal rice for your burrito bowl? Attempt sweet potato. Making sweet potato "rice" is a two-advance procedure. To begin with, cut the sweet potatoes into long slight strands utilizing a spiralizer or vegetable peeler. Then, beat the sweet potato strands into little, ricelike pieces in a nourishment processor.

Fixings 4 servings

2 medium sweet potatoes, stripped 3 tablespoons extra-virgin olive oil, isolated 1 tablespoon bean stew powder 2 teaspoons ground cumin 1 teaspoon garlic powder ¾ teaspoon salt, partitioned 1 pound boneless, skinless chicken bosoms, cut into ½-inch strips 3 cups cut onions (½ inch thick) ¼ cup water ¼ teaspoon ground pepper ½ cup arranged pico de gallo salsa ½ cup destroyed Mexican cheddar mix ¼ cup hacked crisp cilantro Lime wedges for serving.

Arrangement

Position rack in the upper third of broiler. Preheat to 400°F. Utilizing a winding vegetable slicer or a julienne or standard vegetable peeler, cut sweet potatoes longwise into long, slim strands. Whisk 2 tablespoons oil, bean stew powder, cumin, garlic powder and ½ teaspoon salt in an enormous bowl. Include chicken and onions; hurl to cover well. Spread on an enormous rimmed preparing sheet. Broil on the top rack for 12 minutes. In the mean time, place the sweet potato strands in a nourishment processor and heartbeat until about the size of rice grains. Warmth the staying 1 tablespoon oil in a huge nonstick skillet over medium warmth. Include the sweet potato "rice," water, pepper and the remaining ¼ teaspoon salt; cook, blending, until delicate and the water has dissipated, 4 to 6 minutes. After the chicken has cooked for 12 minutes, turn oven on high. Sear until the chicken is cooked through and the onions are sautéed in spots, around 5 minutes more. To serve, place about ¾ cup sweet potato "rice" in every one of 4 shallow dishes. Top with equivalent measures of the chicken-onion blend, salsa, cheddar and cilantro. Present with lime wedges.

Chipotle Chicken Burrito Bowl with Cauliflower Rice
This simple to-make and meal-prep burrito bowl is far and away superior to takeout! You'll never miss the carbs in this protein-pressed, super-delightful meal that replaces the cilantro-lime rice with cauliflower rice. We love this with chicken yet it would be similarly as delightful with shrimp.

Fixings 4 servings
4 cups cauliflower florets 3 tablespoons extra-virgin olive oil, partitioned ½ teaspoon salt, separated 1 pound skinless, boneless chicken bosoms 1 tablespoon finely hacked chipotle peppers in adobo sauce ½ teaspoon garlic powder ½ teaspoon ground cumin 2 cups destroyed romaine lettuce 1 cup canned pinto beans, flushed 1 ready avocado, diced ¼ cup pico de gallo or new salsa ¼ cup destroyed Cheddar or Monterey Jack cheddar Lime wedges for serving.

Planning

Heartbeat cauliflower in a nourishment processor until slashed into rice-size pieces. Warmth 2 tablespoons oil in an enormous skillet over medium-high warmth. Include the cauliflower and ¼ teaspoon salt. Cook, mixing every so often, until the cauliflower is softened, around 5 minutes. Spread and keep warm. Position a rack in upper third of stove; preheat oven to high. Coat an enormous rimmed heating sheet with cooking splash. Season chicken with the remaining ¼ teaspoon salt. Spot on the readied heating sheet and cook for 9 minutes. In the interim, consolidate the staying 1 tablespoon oil, chipotles, garlic powder and cumin in a little bowl. Turn the chicken over, brush with the chipotle coating and keep searing until a moment read thermometer embedded in the thickest part enrolls 165°F, 8 to 10 minutes more. Move to a spotless cutting board and slash into reduced down pieces. Amass each bowl with ½ cup every cauliflower rice, chicken and lettuce, ¼ cup beans, ¼ avocado and 1 tablespoon each pico de gallo (or salsa) and cheddar. Present with a lime wedge.

Hot Slaw Bowls with Shrimp and Edamame

The speedy 10-minute Spicy Cabbage Slaw fills in as the low-carb base in this veggie-stuffed lunch formula. Topped with high-protein edamame and shrimp, this wonderful lunch will assist you with driving through the evening.

Fixings 4 servings

1 formula Spicy Cabbage Slaw (see related formula) 2 cups solidified shelled edamame, defrosted 1 medium avocado, diced ½ medium lime, squeezed 12 ounces stripped cooked shrimp.

Arrangement

Get ready Spicy Cabbage Slaw. Include edamame; hurl and put in a safe spot. Hurl avocado with lime squeeze in a little bowl. Gap the slaw blend among 4 compartments. Top each with ¼ of the shrimp (around 3 ounces) and ¼ of the avocado. Cover and refrigerate until prepared to eat.

To make ahead: Keep cabbage blend and dressing for the Spicy Cabbage Slaw discrete and hold back to join until prepared to eat. If utilizing precooked solidified shrimp, hold on to defrost the shrimp until you're prepared to eat.

Meal-Prep Roasted Vegetable Bowls with Pesto

Your colleagues will be envious when you haul out this healthy lunch of broiled veggies and dark colored rice. Set up together 4 snacks when you have time and you will have packable snacks (or prepared to-eat meals) for a few days—simply snatch a compartment on out the entryway toward the beginning of the day.

Fixings 4 servings

3 tablespoons extra-virgin olive oil, isolated ½ teaspoon garlic powder ¼ teaspoon salt ¼ teaspoon ground pepper 4 cups broccoli florets 2 medium red chime peppers, quartered 1 cup cut red onion 3 cups cooked dark colored rice 1 (15 ounce) can chickpeas, washed 4 tablespoons arranged pesto.

Planning

Preheat broiler to 450°F. Whisk 2 tablespoons oil, garlic powder, salt and pepper together in a huge bowl. Include broccoli, peppers and onion; hurl to cover. Move to an enormous rimmed preparing sheet and meal, blending once, until the vegetables are delicate, around 20 minutes. Slash the peppers when sufficiently cool to deal with. Mix the staying 1 tablespoon oil into rice. Spot about ¾ cup of the rice in every one of four 2-cup microwave-sheltered, lidded holders. Partition chickpeas and the broiled vegetables among the dishes. Top each with 1 tablespoon pesto. To warm: Microwave every holder on High until warmed through, 1 to 2 minutes.

To make ahead: Prepare through Step 3 and refrigerate for as long as 4 days.

Nutty spread Protein Overnight Oats

Powdered nutty spread is a helpful wash room staple that makes an incredible vegetarian protein promoter for oatmeal and smoothies. Twofold or triple this formula to meal-prep morning meals for the week or to eat prepared for the whole family.

Fixings 1 serving

½ cup soymilk or other plant-based milk ½ cup antiquated moved oats (see Tip) 1 tablespoon unadulterated maple syrup 1 tablespoon chia seeds 1 tablespoon powdered nutty spread Pinch of salt ½ medium banana, cut, or ½ cup berries

Arrangement

Prep

Mix soymilk (or other milk)sal, oats, syrup, chia, powdered nutty spread and salt together in a 2-cup artisan container. Refrigerate medium-term. Serve bested with banana or berries.

Tip: People with celiac malady or gluten affectability should utilize oats that are named "sans gluten," as oats are often cross-sullied with wheat and grain.

To make ahead: Prepare through Step 1 and refrigerate for as long as 4 days.

Smooth Blueberry-Pecan Overnight Oatmeal

In this no-cook medium-term oatmeal formula, just rapidly warm the oats in the first part of the day and top with berries, maple syrup and walnuts for a simple, in a hurry breakfast.

Fixings 1 serving

½ cup antiquated moved oats ½ cup water Pinch of salt ½ cup blueberries, new or solidified, defrosted 2 tablespoons nonfat plain Greek yogurt 1 tablespoon toasted hacked walnuts 2 teaspoons unadulterated maple syrup

Arrangement

Consolidate oats, water and salt in a container or bowl. Cover and refrigerate medium-term. In the first part of the day, heat if wanted, and top with blueberries, yogurt, walnuts and syrup.

Individuals with celiac infection or gluten-affectability should utilize oats that are named "sans gluten," as oats are often cross-debased with wheat and grain.

Edamame and Veggie Rice Bowl

The fixings in this vegetarian grain bowl formula can be prepared ahead for a simple lunch to pack for work. The tart citrus dressing is an invigorating flavor with the sweet caramel of the cooked sheet-container veggies.

Fixings 1 serving

½ cup cooked darker rice (see related plans) 1 cup broiled vegetables (see related plans) ¼ cup edamame ¼ avocado, diced 2 tablespoons cut scallions 2 tablespoons cleaved crisp cilantro 2 tablespoons Citrus-Lime Vinaigrette.

Related RECIPES:Easy Brown RiceColorful Roasted Sheet-Pan Veggies Citrus-Lime Vinaigrette

Readiness

Organize rice, veggies, edamame and avocado in a 4-cup sealable holder or bowl. Top with scallions and cilantro. Sprinkle with vinaigrette just before serving.

To make ahead: Refrigerate dressing and bowl independently for as long as 5 days.

Meal-Prep Falafel Bowls with Tahini Sauce

These snappy Mediterranean-enlivened couscous bowls meet up in a short time on account of healthy comfort things like solidified falafel and steam-in-sack crisp green beans. Whisk together the straightforward tahini sauce while different fixings cook.

Fixings 4 servings

1 (8 ounce) bundle solidified arranged falafel ⅔ cup water ½ cup entire wheat couscous 1 (16 ounce) sack steam-in-pack new green beans ½ cup Tahini Sauce (see related formula) ¼ cup set Kalamata olives ¼ cup disintegrated feta cheddar

Arrangement

Get ready falafel as indicated by bundle bearings; put aside to cool. Heat water to the point of boiling in a little pot. Mix in couscous, spread and expel from heat. Permit to remain until the fluid is retained, around 5 minutes. Lighten with a fork; put in a safe spot. Plan green beans as per bundle bearings. Get ready Tahini Sauce. Partition among 4 little sauce holders with covers and refrigerate. Separation the green beans among 4 single-serving compartments with tops. Top each with ½ cup couscous, one-fourth of the falafel and 1 tablespoon every olive and feta. Seal and refrigerate for as long as 4 days. To serve, warm in the microwave until warmed through, around 2 minutes. Dress with tahini sauce just before eating.

To make ahead: Prepare through Step 5; refrigerate fixed holders for as long as 4 days. Warm as coordinated in Step 6.

Vivid Roasted Sheet-Pan Veggies

These simple cooked vegetables will give your plate a fly of shading. Give the solid shapes of butternut squash a head start for 10 minutes to soften in the broiler before including different veggies. The broccoli, peppers and onion are normally more delicate than the butternut squash and cook all the more rapidly. That way everything winds up completing simultaneously.

Fixings 8 servings

3 cups cubed butternut squash (1-inch) 3 tablespoons extra-virgin olive oil, partitioned 4 cups broccoli florets 2 red chime peppers, cut into squares 1 huge red onion, cut into scaled down lumps 2 teaspoons Italian flavoring or herbes de Provence 1 teaspoon coarse genuine salt ¼ teaspoon pepper 1 tablespoon best-quality balsamic vinegar

Readiness

Preheat stove to 425°F. Hurl squash and 1 tablespoon oil in a huge bowl. Spread out on a preparing sheet. Broil for 10 minutes. Then, hurl broccoli, ringer peppers, onion, Italian flavoring (or herbes de Provence), salt and pepper in the bowl with the staying 2 tablespoons olive oil until the vegetables are equitably covered. Add the squash to the vegetables in the bowl. Hurl to consolidate. Spread the vegetables out on 2 heating sheets, partitioning uniformly. Broil, mixing on more than one occasion, until the vegetables are delicate and sautéed in spots, 17 to 20 minutes. Sprinkle with vinegar.

Meal-Prep Cilantro-Lime Chicken Bowls

Prep every one of the four servings of this simple formula on the double for prepared to-eat suppers or packable snacks for the remainder of the week. If you don't care for a ton of warmth, take a stab at utilizing gentle bean stew powder, and forget about the jalapeño from the rice.

Fixings 4 servings

1 pound boneless, skinless chicken bosoms, cut into 1-inch pieces ¾ teaspoon salt, partitioned ½ teaspoon chipotle chile powder or gentle stew powder ¼ teaspoon ground pepper 3 tablespoons extra-virgin olive oil, separated ¼ cup slashed new cilantro 1 medium red onion, cut 1 red chime pepper, cut 1 green ringer pepper, cut 2 cups cooked dark colored rice 1 medium tomato, hacked 1 tablespoon cleaved jalapeño pepper (discretionary) 1 (15 ounce) can decreased sodium dark beans, washed ½ cup disintegrated queso fresco (2½ ounces) 1 lime, cut into 4 wedges.

Readiness

Hurl chicken with ¼ teaspoon salt, chipotle (or bean stew) powder and pepper in a medium bowl. Warmth 2 tablespoons oil in an enormous skillet over medium-high warmth. Include the chicken and cook, mixing at times, until seared and cooked through, 6 to 8 minutes. Move the chicken to a perfect bowl and let cool somewhat. Hurl with cilantro and put in a safe spot. In the meantime, include the staying 1 tablespoon oil to the container. Include onion, red pepper, green pepper and ¼ teaspoon salt. Cook over medium warmth, blending once in a while, until the vegetables have softened and are starting to darker, 6 to 8 minutes. Decrease heat if vegetables are getting excessively dim. Join rice, tomato, jalapeño, if utilizing, and the remaining ¼ teaspoon salt in a medium bowl. To gather: Divide equivalent parts of dark beans, the chicken blend, ringer pepper blend and rice blend among 4 microwave-safe holders. Top each with queso fresco and a lime wedge. Refrigerate until prepared to go through (as long as 4 days). To warm, expel the lime wedge. Microwave every compartment on High for 1 to 2 minutes, or until warmed through. Crush the lime wedge over the top.

To make ahead: Prepare through Step 4 and refrigerate for as long as 4 days.

Cooked Salmon Rice Bowl with Beets and Brussels

Simmering vegetables and salmon together on one sheet dish while the rice cooks makes a simple, fulfilling meal pressed with protein, entire grains and veggies. To guarantee that you're getting 100 percent entire grains, search for a wild rice mix that comprises of wild and dark colored rice.

Fixings 4 servings

1 cup wild rice mix 2 medium brilliant beets, stripped and cut into ½-inch wedges 8 ounces Brussels grows, cut and split 3 tablespoons extra-virgin olive oil, isolated ¾ teaspoon salt, separated ¾ teaspoon ground pepper, partitioned 1 lemon 1 pound wild-got salmon filet, cut into 4 segments 2 rosemary sprigs, cut down the middle 2 tablespoons hacked new herbs, for example, thyme, basil or rosemary 1 clove garlic, minced 1 tablespoon cleaved pistachios

Arrangement

Preheat stove to 425°F. Cook rice mix as per bundle bearings. In the interim, hurl beets and Brussels grows with 1 tablespoon oil and ¼ teaspoon each salt and pepper in a medium bowl. After the rice has cooked for 10 minutes, spread the vegetables on an enormous rimmed preparing sheet and meal until simply starting to dark colored and soften, around 15 minutes. Cut lemon down the middle transversely. Cut a large portion of the lemon into 4 cuts (save the other lemon half). Push the beets and Brussels sprouts to the other side of the heating sheet and spot salmon on the vacant half. Sprinkle the salmon with ¼ teaspoon each salt and pepper and top each bit of salmon with a rosemary sprig and a lemon cut. Keep simmering until the vegetables have softened and the salmon is dark in the middle, 9 to 11 minutes more. In the mean time, crush the juice from the rest of the lemon half into a little bowl. Rush in the staying 2 tablespoons oil, herbs, garlic and the remaining ¼ teaspoon each salt and pepper. Separation the rice among 4 dishes. Dispose of the lemon cuts and rosemary sprig. Orchestrate the salmon and vegetables over the rice. Shower each presenting with around 1 tablespoon lemon juice blend and sprinkle with pistachios.

Zucchini Noodle Bowls with Chicken Sausage and Pesto

Cut down on planning time for this meal-prep zoodle formula by utilizing premade zucchini noodles from the produce segment. Canned beans and precooked chicken wiener heat in around 5 minutes and include protein, while locally acquired refrigerated pesto fills in as a quick and tasty fixing.

Fixings 4 servings

---

2 teaspoons olive oil 6 ounces cooked Italian chicken frankfurter joins (around 2), cut into ½-inch pieces 1 pound zucchini noodles 1 (14 ounce) can no-salt-included cannellini beans, flushed 1 (7 ounce) container simmered red peppers, washed and cut ½ cup refrigerated pesto

Arrangement

Warmth oil in a nonstick skillet over medium warmth. Include frankfurter and cook, blending often, until seared and warmed through, around 5 minutes. Separation zucchini noodles among 4 single-serving compartments with covers (around 2 cups for every holder). Top each with equivalent measures of the frankfurter, beans, peppers and pesto. To warm, vent the top and microwave on High until the hotdog is steaming and the noodles are delicate, 2½ to 3 minutes.

To make ahead: Refrigerate for as long as 4 days.

Meal-Prep Curried Chicken and Chili-Lime Chicken

Spare time and boost your endeavors by stirring up two separate chicken marinades and cooking different plans without a moment's delay. This straightforward yet delightful meal-prep chicken supper thought gives you a chance to cook ahead and not be exhausted with your decisions by mid-week. The two plans are cooked together on a preparing sheet; a foil obstruction keeps them independent. Make this base chicken formula and use it to make the Meal-Prep Chili-Lime Chicken Bowls and Meal-Prep Curried Chicken Bowls (see related plans) for lunch or supper this week.

Fixings 8 servings

Curried Chicken ¾ cup low-fat plain yogurt ⅓ cup ground onion 2 tablespoons gentle curry powder 1½ tablespoons lemon juice 1 tablespoon extra-virgin olive oil ½ teaspoon salt ¼ teaspoon cayenne pepper (discretionary) 1 pound boneless, skinless chicken bosom, cut into 1-inch pieces Chili-Lime Chicken 2 tablespoons extra-virgin olive oil 1 tablespoon bean stew powder 1 teaspoon lime pizzazz 1½ tablespoons lime juice 2 cloves garlic, ground 1 teaspoon ground cumin ½ teaspoon salt 1 pound boneless, skinless chicken bosom, cut into 1-inch pieces

Readiness

To get ready Curried Chicken: Stir yogurt, onion, curry powder, lemon juice, oil, salt and cayenne, if utilizing, together in a medium bowl. Add chicken and hurl to cover. Cover and marinate in the fridge for at any rate 2 hours or medium-term. To get ready Chili-Lime Chicken: Stir oil, stew powder, lime get-up-and-go and squeeze, garlic, cumin and salt together in a medium bowl. Add chicken and hurl to cover. Cover and marinate in the cooler for at any rate 2 hours or medium-term. Preheat broiler to 400°F. Line a rimmed heating sheet with thwart and make a foil obstruction to partition the preparing sheet down the middle. Spot the Curried Chicken, in a solitary layer, on one side of the foil and the Chili-Lime Chicken, in a solitary layer, on the opposite side of the foil. Broil until the chicken is cooked through, 15 to 18 minutes.

To make ahead: Marinate chicken in the cooler as long as 1 day ahead. Refrigerate concocted chicken for to 3 days.

Curried Chicken—Nutrition per ½-cup serving: 198 calories; 7 g fat (2 g sat); 2 g fiber; 7 g starches; 26 g protein; 13 mcg folate; 65 mg cholesterol; 4 g sugar; 0 g included sugar; 40 IU nutrient A; 4 mg nutrient C; 114 mg calcium; 1 mg iron; 380 mg sodium; 357 mg potassium. Sustenance reward: Vitamin B12 (20% day by day esteem). Starch servings: ½; trades: 3 lean protein, 1 fat, ½ vegetable.

Bean stew Lime Chicken—Nutrition per ½-cup serving: 196 calories; 10 g fat (2 g sat); 1 g fiber; 2 g starches; 23 g protein; 4 mcg folate; 63 mg cholesterol; 0 g sugar; 0 g included sugar; 621 IU nutrient A; 3 mg nutrient C; 25 mg calcium; 1 mg iron; 242 mg sodium; 404 mg potassium. Nourishment reward: Vitamin A (69% day by day esteem). Starch servings: 0; trades: 3 lean protein, 1½ fat.

Simple Brown Rice

Here's the main formula you have to make immaculate darker rice without fail! This healthy entire grain is extraordinary all alone as a side dish, or use it in your preferred plans calling for cooked darker rice.

Fixings 6 servings

2½ cups water or juices 1 cup dark colored rice

Planning

Join water (or stock) and rice in a medium pan. Heat to the point of boiling. Diminish warmth to low, spread and stew until delicate and a large portion of the fluid has been ingested, 40 to 50 minutes. Let stand 5 minutes, then cushion with a fork.

To make ahead: Refrigerate cooled rice for as long as 3 days or stop for as long as a half year.

Smooth Vegan Cashew Sauce

You'll never figure this velvety sauce is totally veggie lover, and really produced using pureed cashews. To keep it without gluten, use tamari.

Fixings 8 servings

¾ cup crude cashews ½ cup water ¼ cup stuffed new parsley leaves 1 tablespoon lemon juice or juice vinegar 1 tablespoon extra-virgin olive oil ½ teaspoon diminished sodium tamari or soy sauce ¼ teaspoon salt

Arrangement

Consolidate cashews, water, parsley, lemon juice (or vinegar), oil, tamari (or soy sauce) and salt in a blender. Puree, halting and scratching down the sides as fundamental, until smooth.

To make ahead: Refrigerate for as long as 5 days.

Make-Ahead Smoothie Freezer Packs

Smoothies are an extraordinary healthy breakfast for kids, yet bustling guardians know there's no time for all that slashing and estimating toward the beginning of the day surge. Make these simple DIY smoothie packs early and stash them in your cooler until you're prepared to hum up an organic product filled meal or bite children will adore. This makes enough for a week's worth of work of smoothies!

Fixings 5 servings

2½ cups entire strawberries, blueberries, raspberries or slashed mango, partitioned 2½ cups cut banana, isolated 5 cups unsweetened vanilla almond milk or soymilk, separated

Planning

Spot ½ cup strawberries (or other products of the soil) cup banana in a sealable plastic sandwich pack. Rehash with the rest of the natural product to make 4 additional packs. Store in the cooler until prepared to utilize. To make a smoothie: Place the substance of one pack into a blender alongside 1 cup almond milk (or soymilk). Mix until smooth.

To make ahead: Store smoothie packs in the cooler for as long as 3 months.

Soy-Lime Roasted Tofu

Here we marinate tofu solid shapes in soy sauce and lime juice with a pinch of toasted sesame oil, then dish them—impeccable tofu inevitably.

Fixings 4 servings

2 (14 ounce) bundles extra-firm, water-stuffed tofu, depleted ⅔ cup decreased sodium soy sauce ⅔ cup lime juice 6 tablespoons toasted sesame oil

Planning

Pat tofu dry and slice into ½-to ¾-inch blocks. Join soy sauce, lime squeeze and oil in a medium bowl or huge sealable plastic sack. Include the tofu; tenderly hurl to consolidate. Marinate in the fridge for 1 hour or as long as 4 hours, tenderly blending on more than one occasion. Preheat stove to 450°F. Expel the tofu from the marinade with an opened spoon (dispose of marinade). Spread out on 2 enormous heating sheets, ensuring the pieces are not contacting. Cook, tenderly turning partially through, until brilliant dark colored, around 20 minutes.

To make ahead: Marinate the tofu (Step 1) for as long as 4 hours. Cover and refrigerate broiled tofu for as long as 5 days.

Cut Down on Dishes: A rimmed preparing sheet is extraordinary for everything from simmering to getting unplanned dribbles and spills. For easy cleanup and to keep your heating sheets fit as a fiddle, line them with a layer of foil before each utilization.

Individuals with celiac illness or gluten-affectability should utilize soy sauces that are marked "without gluten," as soy sauce may contain wheat or other gluten-containing sugars and flavors.

Veggie lover Freezer Breakfast Burritos

Having a reserve of delightful spicy burros in your cooler methods you'll generally have a fantastic plant-based meal prepared for a get and-go breakfast on a bustling morning or to take to the campground for a simple pit fire meal. Our vegetarian breakfast filling—made with tofu and arranged to mirror fried eggs—is hurled with beans, veggies and salsa for a delectable and ultra-fulfilling meal.

Fixings 6 servings

2 tablespoons avocado oil, isolated 1 (14 ounce) bundle extra-firm water-stuffed tofu, depleted and disintegrated 2 teaspoons stew powder 1 teaspoon ground cumin ¼ teaspoon salt 1 (15 ounce) can diminished sodium dark beans, washed 1 cup solidified corn, defrosted 4 scallions, cut ½ cup arranged crisp salsa ¼ cup cleaved new cilantro 6 (8 inch) entire wheat tortillas or wraps

Readiness

Warmth 1 tablespoon oil in an enormous nonstick skillet over medium warmth. Include tofu, bean stew powder, cumin and salt; cook, mixing, until the tofu is pleasantly carmelized, 10 to 12 minutes. Move to a bowl. Include the staying 1 tablespoon oil to the dish. Include beans, corn and scallions and cook, blending, until the scallions have softened, around 3 minutes. Return the tofu to the dish. Include salsa and cilantro; cook, mixing, until warmed through, around 2 minutes more. If serving promptly, warm tortillas (or wraps; see Tip), yet if solidifying don't warm them. Gap the bean blend among the tortillas, spreading equally over the base third of every tortilla. Roll cozily, taking care of the closures as you go. Serve promptly or enclose every burrito by foil and stop for as long as 3 months. To warm in the microwave: Remove foil, spread with a paper towel and microwave on High until hot, 1½ to 2 minutes. To warm over a pit fire: Place foil-wrapped burrito on a cooking grate over a medium to medium-hot fire. Cook, turning on more than one occasion, until steaming hot all through, 5 to 10 minutes if somewhat defrosted, as long as 15 minutes if solidified.

To make ahead: Freeze foil-wrapped burritos for as long as 3 months.

Cooked Chickens

In this simple dish chicken formula, two entire winged animals cook next to each other on one skillet, which implies you just need to warm the broiler once yet you'll have enough remaining chicken for quite a long time. Pivoting the chickens on the skillet during simmering guarantees all sides are equally cooked and brilliant dark colored.

Fixings 16 servings

2 5-pound entire chickens, giblets expelled 1 tablespoon fit salt 1 teaspoon ground pepper 1 cup cleaved onion 1 cup slashed celery 1 cup hacked carrot 2 teaspoons extra-virgin olive oil

Arrangement

Dynamic

Preheat stove to 450°F. Coat a huge rimmed heating sheet with cooking shower. Give chickens a chance to remain at room temperature for 30 minutes. Completely pat dry with paper towels, all around. Delicately independent the skin from the meat and season under the skin and inside the hole with salt and pepper. Tie the legs together with kitchen string, for the most part shutting the hole opening. Fold the wing tips under the chickens. Spot onion, celery and carrot on the readied preparing sheet. Brush the chickens with oil and set over the vegetables, around 2 inches separated. Broil in the focal point of the stove for 40 minutes. Utilizing tongs and a spatula to enable you, to pivot every chicken 180 degrees (so the side looking in is presently looking out). Keep cooking until a moment read thermometer embedded into the thickest piece of the thigh, without contacting bone, enlists at any rate 165°F, 20 to 30 minutes more. Tilt every chicken so the juice from the pit runs onto the dish. Move the chickens to a perfect cutting board. Let rest 15 minutes. Expel the string before cutting.

Sheet-Pan Roasted Root Vegetables

One skillet is all you requirement for a stacking heap of nutritious, delicate and brilliant root vegetables. Prepare this huge group formula toward the start of the week to use in simple, healthy meals throughout the entire week.

Fixings 8 servings

2 huge carrots 2 medium parsnips, stripped 2 medium beets, stripped 1 medium red onion 1 medium sweet potato 3 tablespoons extra-virgin olive oil 1½ tablespoons apple juice vinegar or balsamic vinegar 1 tablespoon new herbs, for example, thyme, rosemary or sage ½ teaspoon legitimate salt ½ teaspoon ground pepper

Arrangement

Position racks in upper and lower thirds of stove; preheat to 425°F. Line 2 huge preparing sheets with material paper. Cut carrots and parsnips into ½-inch-thick cuts on a corner to corner, then cut into half-moons. Cut beets and onion into ½-inch-thick wedges. Cut sweet potato into ¾-inch 3D shapes. You ought to have around 12 cups crude vegetables. Hurl the vegetables with oil, vinegar, herbs, salt and pepper in an enormous bowl until all around covered. Partition between the readied heating sheets, spreading into a solitary layer. Broil the vegetables, pivoting the dish start to finish part of the way through, until fork-delicate, 30 to 40 minutes.

To make ahead: Refrigerate cooked vegetables in a water/air proof compartment for as long as 5 days.

Gear: Parchment paper.

Fundamental Quinoa

This secure formula for splendidly cooked quinoa is quick and simple! Utilize cooked quinoa as a straightforward healthy side dish, in a plate of mixed greens or as a base for a delightful primary dish.

Fixings 6 servings

2 cups water or soup 1 cup quinoa

Arrangement

Consolidate water (or juices) and quinoa in a medium pot. Heat to the point of boiling. Lessen warmth to low, spread and stew until delicate and the greater part of the fluid has been retained, 15 to 20 minutes. Cushion with a fork.

To make ahead: Refrigerate for as long as 4 days or stop for as long as 3 months.

Blueberry Almond Chia Pudding

Switch up your morning oatmeal routine with this so-natural chia pudding formula. It's made simply like medium-term oats—consolidate chia and your milk of decision, let drench medium-term, then top with succulent blueberries and crunchy almonds and delve in!

Fixings 1 serving

½ cup unsweetened almond milk or other nondairy milk drink 2 tablespoons chia seeds 2 teaspoons unadulterated maple syrup ⅛ teaspoon almond extricate ½ cup new blueberries, separated 1 tablespoon toasted fragmented almonds, isolated.

Planning

Mix together almond milk (or other nondairy milk refreshment), chia, maple syrup and almond remove in a little bowl. Cover and refrigerate for in any event 8 hours and as long as 3 days. When prepared to serve, mix the pudding admirably. Spoon about a large portion of the pudding into a serving glass (or bowl) and top with a large portion of the blueberries and almonds. Include the remainder of the pudding and top with the rest of the blueberries and almonds.

To make ahead: Refrigerate pudding (Step 1) for as long as 3 days. Finish with Step 2 just before serving.

Hacked Cobb Salad

This single-serving formula for Cobb plate of mixed greens swaps chicken in for bacon, which makes it an incredible wellspring of protein for lunch. If you lean toward another plate of mixed greens dressing, don't hesitate to utilize that rather than our nectar mustard vinaigrette.

Fixings 1 serving

3 cups slashed chunk of ice lettuce 1 cooked chicken thigh, diced (see related formula) 1 stalk celery, diced 1 carrot, diced 1 hard-bubbled egg, diced 1 tablespoon disintegrated blue cheddar 2 tablespoons nectar mustard vinaigrette (see related formula)

Readiness

Organize lettuce, chicken, celery, carrot, egg and blue cheddar in a serving of mixed greens bowl or sealable holder. Prior to serving, sprinkle with dressing.

To make ahead: Asssemble serving of mixed greens and refrigerate for as long as 3 days. Sprinkle with dressing just before serving.

Vegetarian Roasted Vegetable Quinoa Bowl with Creamy Green Sauce

In a vegetarian riff on green goddess dressing, cashews give a velvety base huge amounts of flavor from herbs and apple-juice vinegar. Sprinkle it all over this bowl of quinoa and broiled vegetables to make a fantastic veggie lover supper or simple packable lunch that is prepared in only 30 minutes.

Fixings 4 servings

4 cups broccoli florets 8 ounces cremini mushrooms (3 cups), quartered 2 enormous shallots, cut 2 tablespoons extra-virgin olive oil, partitioned ½ teaspoon salt, separated ¼ teaspoon ground pepper ¾ cup crude cashews ½ cup water ¼ cup crisp parsley leaves 1 tablespoon juice vinegar ½ teaspoon diminished sodium tamari or soy sauce (see Tip) 2 cups cooked quinoa 1 cup destroyed red cabbage.

Planning

Preheat stove to 425°F. Spot broccoli, mushrooms and shallots in a huge bowl. Include 1 tablespoon oil, ¼ teaspoon salt and pepper; hurl to cover. Move to a huge rimmed preparing sheet and dish, mixing once, until the vegetables are delicate and seared, around 20 minutes all out. In the meantime, join cashews, water, parsley, vinegar, tamari (or soy sauce) and the staying 1 tablespoon oil and ¼ teaspoon salt in a blender. Puree, halting and scratching down the sides as essential, until smooth. Partition cooked quinoa, cabbage and the simmered vegetables and sauce among 4 dishes.

Tip: People with celiac sickness or gluten affectability should utilize soy sauces that are named "without gluten," as soy sauce may contain wheat or other gluten-containing fixings.

Biscuit Tin Quiches with Smoked Cheddar and Potato

Potatoes, cheddar and greens make this smaller than usual quiche formula delectable and fulfilling. Heat up a clump throughout the end of the week and you'll eat accessible in a rush for the remainder of the week.

Fixings 6 servings

2 tablespoons extra-virgin olive oil 1½ cups finely diced red-cleaned potatoes 1 cup diced red onion ¾ teaspoon salt, isolated 8 huge eggs 1 cup destroyed smoked cheddar ½ cup low-fat milk ½ teaspoon ground dark pepper 1½ cups hacked new spinach.

Planning

Preheat broiler to 325°F. Coat a 12-cup biscuit tin with cooking splash. Warmth oil in a huge skillet over medium warmth. Include potatoes, onion and ¼ teaspoon salt and cook, mixing, until the potatoes are simply cooked through, around 5 minutes. Expel from warmth and let cool 5 minutes. Whisk eggs, cheddar, milk, pepper and the remaining ½ teaspoon salt in a huge bowl. Mix in spinach and the potato blend. Separation the quiche blend among the readied biscuit cups. Heat until firm to the touch, around 25 minutes. Let stand 5 minutes before expelling from the tin.

To make ahead: Individually envelop by plastic and refrigerate for as long as 3 days or stop for as long as multi month. To warm, evacuate plastic, envelop by a paper towel and microwave on High for 30 to 60 seconds.

Gear: Muffin tin with 12 (½-cup) cups.

Apple Cinnamon Chia Pudding

Switch up your morning oatmeal routine with this so-natural chia pudding formula. It's made simply like medium-term oats: join chia and your milk of decision, let splash medium-term, then top with the exemplary flavor combo of apples and cinnamon, with walnuts for included crunch.

Fixings 1 serving

½ cup unsweetened almond milk or other nondairy milk 2 tablespoons chia seeds 2 teaspoons unadulterated maple syrup ¼ teaspoon vanilla concentrate ¼ teaspoon ground cinnamon ½ cup diced apple, partitioned 1 tablespoon slashed toasted walnuts, separated.

Planning

Mix almond milk (or other nondairy milk), chia, maple syrup, vanilla and cinnamon together in a little bowl. Cover and refrigerate for in any event 8 hours and as long as 3 days. When prepared to serve, mix well. Spoon about a large portion of the pudding into a serving glass (or bowl) and top with a large portion of the apple and walnuts. Include the remainder of the pudding and top with the rest of the apple and walnuts. To make ahead: Refrigerate pudding (Step 1) for as long as 3 days. Finish with Step 2 just before serving.

Meal-Prep Sheet-Pan Chicken Thighs

Concoct six servings of chicken without a moment's delay with this speedy and simple meal-prep formula: you'll have formula prepared cooked chicken in the ice chest for put together snacks and suppers consistently. This straightforward sheet-dish chicken thigh formula gets a simple eruption of flavor from dried oregano and a clove of garlic.

Fixings 6 servings

1¾ pounds boneless, skinless chicken thighs, cut 2 teaspoons extra-virgin olive oil 1 enormous clove garlic, minced 1 teaspoon fit salt 1 teaspoon dried oregano.

Readiness

Preheat broiler to 425°F. Line a heating sheet with material paper. Spot chicken in a huge bowl. Include oil, garlic, salt and oregano; hurl until all around covered. Orchestrate the chicken on the readied skillet. Broil until cooked through, 18 to 22 minutes.

To make ahead: Refrigerate for as long as 3 days or stop for as long as 3 months.

Tip: See how to meal-prep this formula and an entire week of suppers with this plan.

CONCLUSION

Who hasn't gone home late with a snarling stomach however little vitality to shop and cook? A bustling timetable is one of the top reasons why individuals pick snappy takeout meals, which are often calorie-loaded and a supporter of extending waistlines.

Presently, envision a different situation where inside a couple of moments of strolling through the entryway you have a delectable home-prepared supper, and maybe even lunch stuffed up for the following day. In the midst of riotous weekday plans, meal prep or meal planning is an incredible apparatus to help keep us on a healthy eating track. Albeit any sort of meal prep requires planning, there is nobody right strategy, as it can differ dependent on nourishment inclinations, cooking capacity, calendars, and individual objectives. Here are a few models:

If you presently eat cheap food or takeout a few evenings of the week, your objective might be to pick a specific day of the week to make a nourishment shopping rundown and hit the market.

If you as of now nourishment shop once every week and have fundamental cooking abilities, your objective might be to pick one day seven days to do a large portion of the cooking, or attempt another formula.

If you as of now cook some weekday meals for your family, you may choose to make a timetable with the goal that you are not choosing a minute ago what to make and to guarantee you have the required fixings close by.

A few advantages of meal prep:

Can help set aside cash

Can eventually spare time

Can help with weight control, as you choose the fixings and parts served

Can add to a general all the more healthfully adjusted eating routine

Can decrease worry as you maintain a strategic distance from a minute ago choices about what to eat, or surged readiness

Preparing for Meal Prep

Talk about with your family what sorts of nourishments and most loved meals they like to eat.

Start a month to month schedule or spreadsheet to record your meal thoughts, most loved formula locales, and nourishment shopping records.

Gather healthy plans. Clasp plans from print magazines and papers and spare in a fastener, or duplicate connections of plans onto an online spreadsheet.

Think about specific meals or nourishments for different days of the week. Recall Wednesday as Prince Spaghetti Day? A few families appreciate the consistency of recognizing what's in store, and it can facilitate your meal planning. Models are Meatless Mondays, Whole Grain Wednesdays, Stir-Fry Fridays, and so on.

Start little: Aim to make enough meals for 2-3 days of the week.

Beginning

Case of a meal readiness calendar. Choose a specific day of the week to: 1) plan the menu, regardless of whether step by step or for the entire month, and work out your basic food item list 2) nourishment shop, 3) do meal prep, or the greater part of your cooking. A portion of nowadays may cover if you pick, yet separating these errands may help keep meal planning reasonable.

As you discover top choice 'prep-capable' meals, or your menus become increasingly well-known and predictable, watch for deals and coupons to load up on as often as possible utilized rack stable fixings like pasta, rice, and other entire grains, lentils, beans (canned or dried), bumped sauces, healthy oils, and flavors.

On your meal prep day, center first around nourishments that take the longest to cook: proteins like chicken and fish; entire grains like dark colored rice, quinoa, and farro; dried beans and vegetables; and, broiled vegetables.

Likewise consider getting ready staple nourishments that everybody in the family appreciates and which you can without much of a stretch add to a weekday meal or get for a bite: washed greens for a serving of mixed greens, hardboiled eggs, a bowl of slashed natural product, cooked beans.

If you incline toward not to pre-cook proteins, consider marinating poultry, fish, or even tofu on your prep day with the goal that you can rapidly pop them into the broiler or sautéed food later in the week.

Perform various tasks! While nourishments are heating or rising on the stovetop, hack vegetables and new organic product, or wash and dry serving of mixed greens for later in the week.

When you cook a formula, make additional bits for one more day or two of meals, or to solidify for a different week. Make certain to date and name what goes in the cooler so you recognize what you have close by.

For snacks, get a head-start and utilize singular meal compartments. Partition prepared nourishment into the compartments on prep day.

CPSIA information can be obtained
at www.ICGtesting.com
Printed in the USA
BVHW092022190421
605310BV00004B/311